ADAM'S U

Written by
RAHAF KANAAN

Design by
Saher Mushtaq

DEDICATION

This book is a dedication to my wonderful family and all the children of the world.

IT WAS BED TIME FOR LITTLE ADAM.

ADAM WAS A LITTLE GRAY AND WHITE YOUNG RABBIT WHO LOVED TO HAVE FUN.

As he was playing with his toy, he heard his dad's voice.

"IT'S TIME FOR YOU TO GET READY FOR BED ADAM" SAID DAD SMILING.

"I WANT TO PLAY! AND WISH MY DAD TO GO AWAY." SHOUTED ADAM.
"FAR AWAY TO THE MOON I SAY," FROWNED THE LITTLE RABBIT.

HIS WISH WAS GRANTED IN MANY FEARS. ADAM'S EYES WERE FILLED WITH TEARS.

GRANDPA WALKED IN THE ROOM AND SAW ADAM CRYING.

"IT'S OK LITTLEONE," SAID HIS GRANDPA CUDDLING ADAM.

HE TOOK HIM TO SEE HIS DAD ALL THE WAY UP, UP, UP TO THE MOON.

THERE WAS DAD SITTING VERY SAD.

THE LITTLE RABBIT RAN AND GAVE A BIG HUG TO HIS DAD. HE PROMISED TO BE A GOOD BOY.

DAD LIFTED ADAM UP IN THE AIR AND SAID, "I LOVE YOU MY LITTLEONE."

THEN GRANDPA, DAD AND ADAM ZOOMED BACK HOME.

GETTING READY FOR BED THE LITTLE RABBIT BRUSHED HIS TEETH.

HE CLEANED HIS ROOM.

"GOODNIGHT LITTLEONE," SAID DAD.

TUCKED IN BED, ADAM SMILED AND SAID "MY DAD IS THE BEST, A TREASURE TO KEEP."
THEN HE FELL FAST ASLEEP.

Answer these questions Kids

* Did Adam get his wish?

* Where was Adam's dad?

* Why was the little rabbit sad?

* Who got a big hug?

Let us color Adam

Let us color Adam's Father

Let us color Adam's Grandfather

Made in the USA
Columbia, SC
30 October 2020